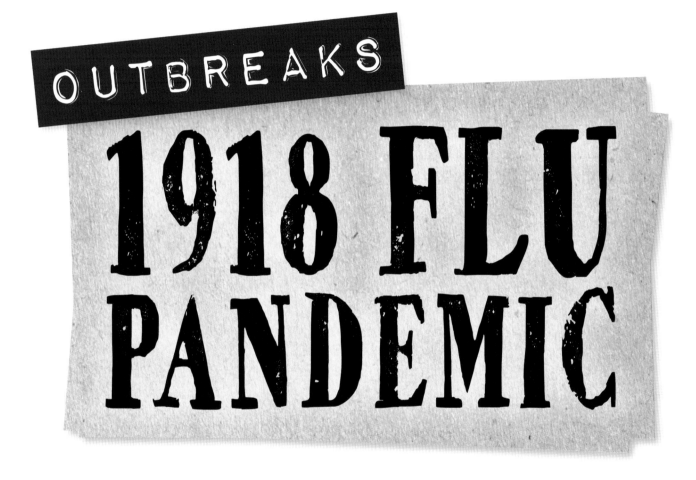

OUTBREAKS

1918 FLU PANDEMIC

BY JOHN WOOD

BookLife
PUBLISHING

©2022
BookLife Publishing Ltd.
King's Lynn
Norfolk, PE30 4LS, UK

All rights reserved.
Printed in Poland.

A catalogue record for this book
is available from the British
Library.

ISBN: 978-1-83927-689-7

Written by:
John Wood

Edited by:
Madeline Tyler

Designed by:
Jasmine Pointer

All facts, statistics, web addresses
and URLs in this book were verified
as valid and accurate at time of
writing. No responsibility for any
changes to external websites or
references can be accepted by
either the author or publisher.

Image Credits

CONTENTS

Words that look like **this** can be found in the glossary on page 24.

SPREADING
SICKNESS

We share our world with lots of tiny things that are too small to see. Some of these things help us, but some of these things are dangerous and can make people ill.

We can use a _microscope_ like this...

... to see tiny things like this.

Some illnesses are caused by tiny things called viruses. Viruses get into a person's body and make more of themselves. Other illnesses can be caused by **bacteria**.

Virus

When many people get ill from one type of bacteria, it is sometimes called a plague.

OUTBREAKS

When lots of people get an illness, it is called an outbreak. There are different types of outbreaks.

Epidemic: When a disease <u>spreads</u> quickly in part of a place or part of the world

Pandemic: When a disease spreads quickly over a whole country or the whole world

Because it is easy to travel and send things around the world, it means diseases can easily spread a long way too.

We are all very connected to each other.

A WORLD WITH FLU

The 1918 flu killed more people than any other outbreak of flu in history. It is a virus, and it **infected** around 500 million people. It is thought that up to 50 million died.

These soldiers are wearing masks to stop the spread of the virus in 1918.

This is a map that shows which countries had the most deaths between 1918 and 1920.

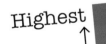

Highest

Lowest

Not Known

ILL WITH THE 1918 FLU

In some ways, the 1918 flu was a lot like the flu today. People might vomit and get a fever. Their body might also ache in places.

People with a fever feel very hot.

People might also have runny poo. This is also known as diarrhoea.

However, the 1918 flu was much deadlier than normal flu. Unlike other viruses, this one was worst for young, healthy people, especially people between 20 and 30 years old.

It is thought that one in ten people who caught it died.

This is a hospital <u>ward</u> during the pandemic.

There are lots of different kinds of flu. Different kinds of the same disease are called strains. The 1918 flu strain was called H1N1. It is thought that this strain came from birds.

H1N1 : - ☐ + ☑

Since the H1N1 strain, there have been more viruses that are similar to H1N1.

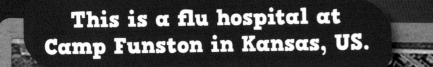

This is a flu hospital at Camp Funston in Kansas, US.

Nobody is sure exactly where the 1918 outbreak began. However, many people now think it probably started in the US.

HOW THIS FLU
TRAVELLED

In 1918, many countries in the world were fighting a war against each other. This was called World War One. This war made the virus much worse for people.

Soldiers caught the virus and then moved around the world, spreading it to lots of different countries. The camps that the soldiers stayed in were also small and cramped, meaning lots of people caught it and died.

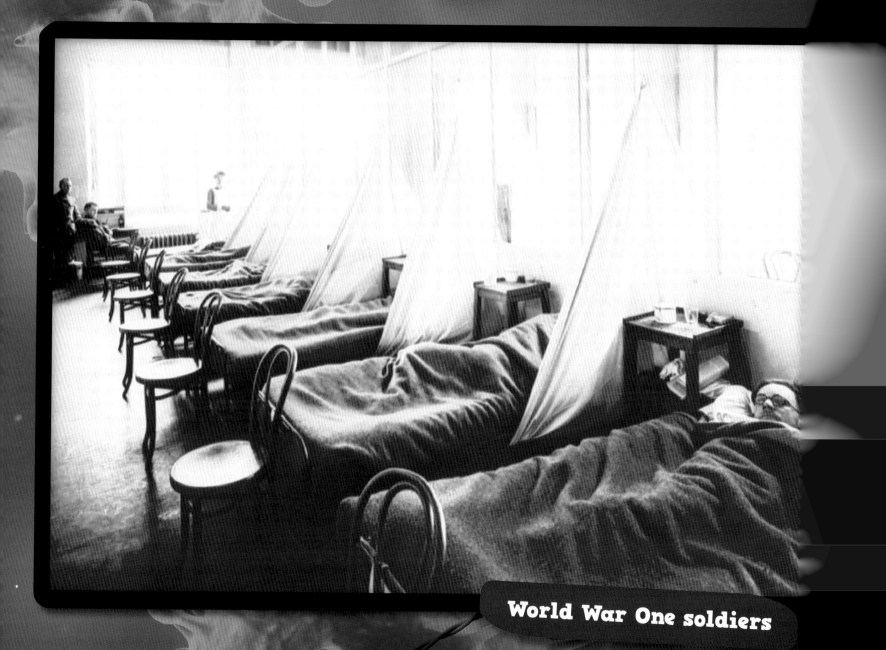

World War One soldiers

INDIA

India was hit the hardest by the 1918 pandemic. It is thought that between 12 to 18 million people died in India, which is more than in any other country.

India

People were already weak and underfed because a _drought_ had made it harder to grow food.

At the time, India was **ruled** by Britain. However, the British **government** did not care about looking after the people of India. This meant there were not enough doctors and hospitals to help fight the 1918 flu.

These people are protesting British rule in India. British people in charge treated the Indian people very badly.

PANDEMIC AND WAR

Lots of doctors and health workers were helping with the war and were not able to treat the sick.

A <u>temporary</u> flu hospital

Not only did World War One help spread the flu, but it also made it harder to fight against the disease. This was because a lot of effort was going into fighting the war.

During the war, many countries didn't talk about the flu because they didn't want their enemies to think they were weak. This meant that many people didn't realise how serious the disease was.

Daily Net SALE Six Times as Large as That of Any Penny London Morning Journal Except "THE TIMES"

MBER 31, 1914   LONDON   MANCHESTER   PARIS   NO 5,848

OW TO FIGHT A VIRUS

A vaccine is an injection that is given to people to stop them getting ill from certain diseases. Vaccines are a good way of fighting viruses, but no vaccine had been found to stop the 1918 flu.

There was also no medicine to treat any <u>infections</u> that happened because of the flu.

This meant that countries did other things to stop the disease, such as washing things a lot or telling people not to meet in groups. However, not everyone did this, which made the disease worse.

This family photo was taken during the 1918 pandemic.

THE END OF THE PANDEMIC

Schools, shops and restaurants closed around the world. People were asked to not meet up with each other.

The 1918 flu spread through the world for a few years before going away in the early 1920s. This is because most of the people left were **immune** to the virus by then.

Washing our hands and not meeting up with other people are often the best ways to fight a dangerous virus when there is no cure. By doing this we can all stay safe.

GLOSSARY

bacteria	tiny living things, too small to see, that can cause diseases
drought	a long time without rainfall, which leads to a lack of water
government	the people in charge of a country who decide the rules everybody lives by
immune	protected from a disease and not made ill by it
infected	ill from dirt or things such as bacteria or viruses getting into the body
infections	illnesses caused by dirt, germs and bacteria getting into the body
microscope	a piece of scientific equipment that makes things look many times bigger
ruled	controlled by
spreads	moves to other areas
temporary	only lasting for a short time
ward	a room or area in a hospital

INDEX